First of the
Summer Wine

Hazel Wheeler

MRM Associates Limited,
Unit C4, Weldale Street,
Reading, Berkshire RG1 7BX

ISBN 0 9517718 8 1

Distributed through
Local Heritage Books,
Highfield House, 2 Highfield Avenue,
Newbury, Berkshire RG14 5DS

Contents

Foreword

More than thirty years ago a production unit of the Comedy Department of BBC Television descended upon the West Yorkshire town of Holmfirth to begin filming scenes for a new situation comedy provisionally entitled 'Last of the Summer Wine' although all concerned assumed that such an unlikely sitcom title would soon be changed for something better.

Fate, and the town's dramatically beautiful setting among the hills and valleys, had led to the selection of Holmfirth as the ideal location for the new programme. At that time the town was quietly minding its own business and few expected that the BBC intrusion would be a long one. There was perhaps even a feeling among the unit that if people didn't like the show at least they could enjoy the scenery.

And enjoy it they did. They came to look at it in the green and pleasant 'flesh' and they're still coming – often now from very far – with the result that the link between the programme and the area is now so well established that it's easy to overlook the town's much earlier claims to a place in the history of popular culture. Hazel Wheeler's book goes a long way towards restoring the balance by a very detailed and attractively anecdotal account of those earlier years.

When the BBC fell upon it in 1972 that quiet, cagey, undemonstrative town was already secure of its contribution to the early days of film. In typical local fashion it made no fuss about it. You practically had to pull fingernails before people would talk about it, but there in the heart of town, still quietly beavering away, was Bamforth's. For the older generations a part of everyone's past. If you're ever laughed at a saucy postcard at the seaside the chances are it was one of Bamforth's. And just how much more there was to Bamforth's is clearly shown by Hazel Wheeler's researches into these fascinating times.

Sobering for the Young Turks of the film unit that came late to the town was the fact that, before the First World War, Holmfirth was making short, silent films the equal of anything that was coming from America at that time. These hills might never have been the Hollywood Hills, but who knows how large a name might have been built here on those inspired, early efforts if the war hadn't deprived them of all access to film stock and other essential materials?

This is their story told – not as some dry, scholarly exercise but – with the author's own memories giving her insight into and great empathy with the lives of those of whom she writes. Marion Barrowclough telling her story to the author.

I recommend this book as a tribute to some remarkable people in a remarkable place at a fascinating time.

Roy Clarke

Introduction
(Acknowledgments to Bamforth's)

Even as far back as 1870, the hilly Yorkshire town of Holmfirth was destined for fame. Long before 'Last of the Summer Wine' Compo, Nora Batty, and the rest of that lot who made the area world famous arrived on the scene, Bamforths almost beat Hollywood to film fame.

That 'certain something' that singles Holmfirth and its inhabitants out from more sophisticated types was evident then. How? Few will not have bought a Bamforth of Holmfirth comic or view postcard while on holiday. But prior to those, James Bamforth established the family firm using his ability as an artist to paint backgrounds for thousands of Life Model Lantern slides he produced in the latter years of the 19th century.

His other interest was photography. Those slides were made to illustrate lovely sentimental song and hymn cards. Usually in sets of three or four, therefore if all the verses were wanted, all the postcards had to be bought.

In 1902 postcard collecting was all the rage. The last owner of the firm, Derek, continued his father Edwin's work of producing postcards from the existing lantern slides, depicting the popular songs of the day.

Wonderful words and tunes which will still be sung when the banal 'pop' stuff now infiltrating every aspect of life will have been long forgotten.

James Bamforth, the founder of the Company.

Derek Bamforth, the last family member to run the business.

Titles such as 'When You Come Home,' 'The Trail of The Lonesome Pine,' 'Roamin' in the Gloamin','' 'Seated One Day At The Organ,' 'I Hear You Calling Me,' 'My Hero' to name but a few.

The latter, from 'The Chocolate Soldier' has words almost forgotten today. More's the pity.

In Old People's Homes memories can still be stirred by singing 'I'm Forever Blowing Bubbles', 'The Magic of Your Voice' and hymns 'O Love That Wilt Not Let Me Go' 'Brightly Gleams Our Banner' and 'Abide With Me.' Only a few of the many by Bamforths, illustrated by local Holmfirth people posing for them, the verses printed beneath.

And still available at Postcard Societies throughout the country, or in antique shops.

If only they could be more promoted instead of the monotonous diet of sex and violence-no need for drugs when listening to 'When You Come Home' – capturing the essence of what home life should, ideally be.

My grateful thanks to Bamforths for permission to use these wonderful postcards.

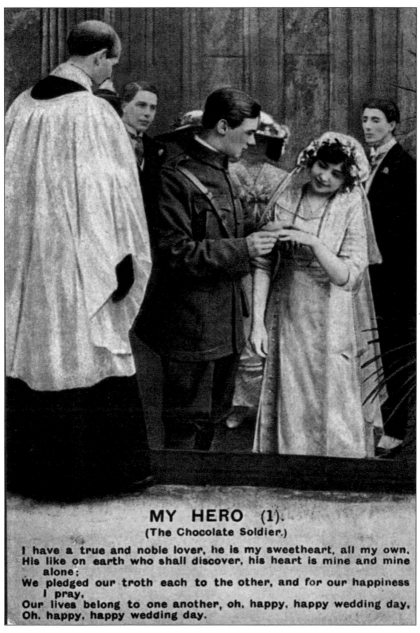

MY HERO (1).
(The Chocolate Soldier.)

I have a true and noble lover, he is my sweetheart, all my own.
His like on earth who shall discover, his heart is mine and mine
    alone;
We pledged our troth each to the other, and for our happiness
    I pray,
Our lives belong to one another, oh, happy, happy wedding day,
Oh, happy, happy wedding day.

Marriage – which usually lasted – 'Till Death do us Part'.

When song was sweet –

'Take Me Back to Dear Old Blighty' shows local chaps dressed in khaki, posing against a painted backcloth of a dug out. While that evergreen 'It's a Long Way to Tipperary' and 'I'll Take You Home Again Kathleen' superbly capture the mood of the time.

Bamforths were noted for humour as well as pathos. The latter title shows a fellow pushing a drunk past a public house in a wheelbarrow.

So successful were these postcards that offices were opened in London and New York. Many of the postcards were in sepia, later beautifully reproduced in colour. Had there been a competition in those days for the most beautiful girl in the world, Hannah Hinchliffe, a Holmfirth weaver, would surely have won it.

Before the first world war when Marion Leake, (who's story is told in this book,) was a child, Hannah was a beautiful young lady who featured on many postcards What quirks of fate alter our lives –

Hannah, born in 1887, worked in Bottoms mill when she was invited to pose for Bamforths. Hers was not the only beauty to enhance those sentimental song cards, she had three sisters, Martha, Lily and Edith, who also were used. But Hannah the most. Appearing on 'The Lost Chord', 'Sun of My Soul', 'She Wore a Wreath of Roses', 'Nazareth', 'Lead, Kindly Light' and many others. Hannah had perfect features and a lovely figure.

When Hannah's fame was at its height Bamforths were involved in a court case with a gentleman in America. The outcome being that Bamforths took their 'Star' model out to America to prove that she was their own 'property'. The firm won the case and Hannah returned to Holmfirth. If her mother had allowed her daughter to stay in America, as Hannah wanted to do, the name of Hannah Hinchliffe may well have been as famous as that of Greta Garbo or Mary Pickford.

So Hannah married Fred Taylor of Holmfirth and lived at the bottom of South Lane there. Fred owned a garage, and all ideas of life and film fame in the U.S.A flew out of the window when the couple produced two sons and a daughter. Who turned out to be as beautiful as her mother. Girls like Hannah used no make-up, wore decorous clothing, attended church regularly-and obviously did as their parents told them! It must have been like living on a different planet.

Simplicity and innocence proved the winning ingredient in the success of those postcards. The local people who posed for Bamforths did it 'to oblige' and for fun, certainly not for gain. Being highly delighted if given a set of photographs, and threepence (in old money.)

Bamforths had a brief success producing comedy films, and were the first firm in the country to make films for public exhibition on a commercial basis in 1899 A local French polisher, Fred Beaumont, became their first ever film comedian as he starred in a series of silent 'shorts.' Later developing a tramp character. (Shades of 'Compo' in the future?) Another 'local' comedian was an eccentric gentleman known as Winky, played by Reginald Switz 'Winky' who became star of more than fifty comedy shorts between 1913 and 1915. He became nationally known, and an order for a hundred silent movies was received by Bamforths from Russia.

Titles of Winky's successes are a parallel with titles of 'Last of the Summer Wine.' 'Winky Learns a lesson in Honesty.' 'Winky and The Gorgonzola Cheese.' 'Winky and the Leopard.'

Easy to picture Bill Owen, 'Compo' in those roles!

Those silent films were regularly screened at Holmfirth Postcard Museum before it was closed by Kirklees Council in 1997. Who then proposed to put Bamforth postcards on display in Holmfirth Valley Cinema. Which was opened by comedian Norman Wisdom (One time news reader Ian McCaskill opened the Postcard Museum in 1987.)

When the first world war intervened, Bamforths were streets ahead of America in production methods and technique Insuperable difficulties arose, celluloid was needed to make explosives, and movie making in the Holme Valley ceased. Two of their cameramen were 'snapped up' by Pathe Gazette.

If the war stopped the film enterprise, it gave a boost to the money making business of Life Form Picture Postcards. Posed by local people, illustrating popular songs of the day and sent to soldiers fighting for King and Country. Thousands of cards were

IT'S A LONG, LONG WAY TO TIPPERARY (2).

"It's a long way to Tipperary, it's a long way to go;
It's a long way to Tipperary, to the sweetest girl
    I know;
Good-bye Piccadilly, farewell Leicester Square,
It's a long, long way to Tipperary, but my heart's
    right there."

BANFORTH (Copyright)

THIS SONG ON SALE EVERYWHERE IN B. FELDMAN'S 6D. EDITIONS.

Many cards depicted popular songs of the day.

JESU, LOVER OF MY SOUL (3).

Plenteous grace with Thee is found,
  Grace to cleanse from every sin;
Let the healing streams abound,
  Make and keep me pure within.
Thou of life the fountain art,
  Freely let me take of Thee;
Spring Thou up within my heart;
  Rise to all eternity.

Hannah Hinchliffe, a local weaver, was one of Bamforths most beautiful models.

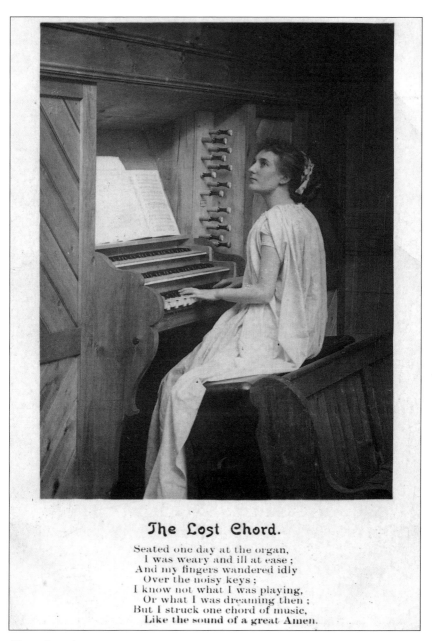

The Lost Chord.

Seated one day at the organ,
I was weary and ill at ease;
And my fingers wandered idly
Over the noisy keys;
I know not what I was playing,
Or what I was dreaming then;
But I struck one chord of music,
Like the sound of a great Amen.

Hannah again.

Marion Barrowclough (nee Leake) visits the Bamforth Factory.

posted, at the height of their popularity Bamforths was printing 20 million cards a year for export round the world.

There must have been enough tears shed during that time to sink battleships. One illustrated ditty being 'Don't Go Down The Mine, Dad.' The story of a young boy who dreams of a pit disaster and pleads with his father not to go to work. The father is saved, but 20 of his colleagues die in an underground fire.

Such postcards continued until 1918 when the war ended. Sadly, sentiment died with it and millions of postcards were destroyed. How fortunate that many were hoarded in attics and cupboards, becoming collectors' items in later years.

After the stress of war years the British public yearned for laughter. Bamforths responded, giving the world saucy seaside postcards. And newsagents stands, especially in seaside resorts, where holiday makers twirled the cards round picking out the most apt for friends back home, then sitting on deckchairs to pen 'Wish You Were Here' scribbles in pencil.

Douglas Tempest was one of the first to draw saucy postcards.

I CAN TELL IT'S YOU, GEORGE; YOU SMELL OF HAY—YOU'VE BEEN SMOKING THOSE NASTY WOODBINES AGAIN!

Then it was that artists came into their own. Douglas Tempest joined the firm in 1911, one of the first to specialize in saucy postcards. Others being Donald McGill, Brian Fitzpatrick, and Arnold Taylor. Arnold lived near Holmfirth all his life, apart from serving in the Western Desert during the second world war. After demob he worked as illustrator for the army magazine Parade. Later as book illustrator in London, producing covers for books by Dennis Wheatley, Agatha Christie, and John Creasey.

But the pull of home and Holmfirth was too strong, and Arnold worked for Bamforths creating comic postcards until he retired.

The first card he drew was of a large woman alongside a henpecked little man. 'I'm going to have pneumonia lass,' he says. Her caption being 'You're having nowt 'til I've had a new hat.' A typical conversation Taylor probably overheard on Holmfirth's cobbled streets.

Tempest was with the firm forty years. Nothing beats working for a family firm! Cards those artists produced reflected the era they lived through. The Jazz Age of the Twenties, 'flappers' and short skirts. In the 30's the emphasis was on healthy hiking and seaside 'hols.' While patriotic themes featured during the war.

Bamforths turned out 16 million picture postcards a year in the 1960's. But in 1987 the firm was bought by Dennis, Print and Publishing of Scarborough. By 1990 sales were slipping, postcard illustration was taken over by the Scarborough firm, the Holmfirth premises then only used for producing calendars.

Already those halcyon days of bustle and film making in the Holme Valley were becoming a fast fading memory. Days when anyone out shopping or simply for a walk could be roped in as a film extra. Taken by wagonette to location 'shoots' such as local beauty spots Hope Bank Pleasure Ground, gardens at Honley, or to Beaumont Park near Huddersfield. Places that have featured in Last of the Summer Wine episodes. Written by Roy Clarke. (The Yorkshire feller who invented 'Compo' and Co.putting Holmfirth firmly on the entertainment map once again.)

Bill Owen, 'Compo' now resides where he wanted his final earthly resting place to be, in a Holmfirth churchyard. There are

Arnold Taylor, one of Bamforth's most popular artists.

One of Arnold Taylor's trademark cards.

horse drawn tours round Holmfirth still, and the tourist boom continues. While the owner of the Toll House bookshop says any book about Holmfirth sells like hot dinners!

How proud Marion, Hannah, and the other Bamforth models would have been to be part of that happy heritage.

Quite apart from the pleasure to be derived from the songs and illustrations of Bamforth postcards, what amusement and social history there is in the messages on the backs of some.

On the back of 'I Heard The Voice of Jesus Say' Lily wrote in 1910, 'Dear M.I had a glorious time yesterday went to the dentist had 8 teeth drawn going today to have another drawn. byking to Rotherham.'

Postmarked November 4th. 1909 to Miss Phipps, Broad Oak, Accrington, Lancashire. 'Dear S. will you please send my fur as it is getting very cold here I think I left it in your wardrobe. I hope you are all well as it leaves me pretty well at present. With love to all from M.A.' (Message on the back of 'If you Please, Miss, Give Me Heaven.')

Hope Bank Pleasure Ground at Honley.

leasure Ground, Hope Bank Pleasure Gardens, Honley Nr. Huddersfield.

A pencilled few lines on the back of 'Just As The Sun Went Down' (a halfpenny stamp,) 'Dear Mary I have promised you a postcard long enough so I thought I make my words good. Excuse writing got cramp in big toe. From Agnes. P.S. Short and sweet as a donkey's trot.' (You can't keep a telephone call for decades, and to hand down to descendants.)

In April 1909 Miss Lenore Murphy received a postcard showing the child Marion Leake in 'Gentle Jesus' pose, sitting up in bed in her flannelette nightie. On the back 'Dear Daughter, I received your cards today, my cold is better will be alright in a day or two. Ella Dooley came near dying with convulsions but she has a young son and is better. Be careful the kind of place you get into in St. Paul. Write to me if you don't come home now.'

Ethel wrote to Fred on February 16th 1910 that she was 'up to the eyes in Spring cleaning.' But hoped to be going over to Harrogate that weekend as it was her Sunday out.

In the days when ladies stayed at home after marriage much time was spent in dressmaking. A dressmaker's model like the one on the card captioned 'Walse me around again Willie' was a normal feature in many households.

Many of the male population were named Fred in those days. Private Fred Plummer was in the Royal Victoria Hospital in 1916 when his 'loving wife and daughter' posted him a Bamforth comic 'Dreamland' postcard, stamped with the green halfpenny stamp.

Before the popular use of wireless came into vogue, singing round the piano boosted the sale of song sheets. Lots of words on them now out of normal usage. How many today would know what to reply if someone accosted them and asked 'How'd you like to Spoon with me?' Nor would the modern disco loving girl think she had been taken out if all that it entailed was sitting on a fence beneath a big moon and 'spooning.'

The Bamforth family often dressed up and acted 'daft' for some of their postcards. 'When I was Sweet Sixteen' has Teddy Bamforth as the simpering 'girl.' Teddy being the family name for Edwin.

What marvellous actors and actresses those Holmfirth folk were, considering most of them never had an acting lesson in their lives!

19

The Bamforth Family often appeared in the cards.

ONE

Story of Marion, A Pre First World War Bamforth Postcard Model

Life models for Bamforths of Holmfirth, who produced tear-jerking, sentimental song and hymn cards in the first half of the 20th. Century, were as natural as the homes from whence they sprang.

Quite without artifice or sophistication, the stone cottages and homesteads which seemingly grew out of the steep hillsides, in a way resembled the people who lived there. Made to withstand the rigours of real life, to plumb the worst -and best-of the elements and emotions.

Holmfirth, then the hub of the Postcard Industry, is, on the face of it, the last kind of locality to achieve world wide fame. A tightly knit community, where everyone knew everybody else, before the tourist industry of modern times as a result of the T.V. series Last of the Summer Wine.

A small West Yorkshire town surrounded by extraordinarily steep hills with winding, cobbled paths-many still are-and a road down into Huddersfield. Hamlets dotted the summits of hills, rugged and resolute, with no necessity for adornment. Frills and furblows would 'look daft' amid such natural wild grandeur.

Such was the landscape that bred the men, women, and children selected by the local Bamforth photographic family to pose for their postcards, hymn cards and calendars. No need for professional training or Drama Schools. The eyes of Frank Bamforth could tell at a glance who would be right for his child studies.

One ideal subject, in pre-world war one days, was Marion Leake. Born on 23rd. February 1900 to Sarah and Sydney. The

PLEASE GIVE ME A PENNY (1).

Please give me a penny, sir,
My mother dear is dead,
And oh! I am so hungry, sir,
A penny please for bread,
All day I have been asking,
But no one heeds my cry.
Will you not give me something?
Or surely I must die.
Chorus: Oh! please give me a penny, sir,
My mother dear is dead,
And oh! I am so hungry, sir,
A penny please for bread.

Marion Leake, a popular Bamforth model.

couple already had one daughter, Nellie, a son, Ernest, and Marion's half-brother Herbert. Gilbert followed two years later.

Sydney toiled in Newgate Quarry for $3\frac{1}{2}$d (old money) an hour, but loved the freedom of the outdoors. Life, though, was hard in those days, with no social security to cushion one against the bad times, and wages depended entirely on the weather. In 1900 there was a prolonged frost, and lots of families where the bread earner depended on hewing stone in Newgate simply couldn't manage. No work, no wages, was the accepted way of life then. Soup kitchens were opened in Holmfirth, but the Leake family were too proud to visit them-and Sarah had a bit of money 'put by' of her own, which tided them over until the better weather returned.

Apart from the loss of work it was a tragic year in other ways for the family. Sarah's sister-in-law, who lived in the cottage next door with her husband and children, became blind. So Sarah took it upon herself to care for them as well as her own children.

To make matters even worse, little Ernest took to his bed with scarlet fever. There were no isolation hospitals then for the four-year-old to be cared for in, and despite the utmost care, love and devotion from his mother, he died, and was buried in the churchyard.

What an upheaval that created in the Leake household. Everything in the house had to be 'stoved' and until that was done none of the family was allowed to mingle with anyone else, to minimise the risk of further infection.

That day Sarah gathered together her own and her sister-in-law's children and all of them set out to trudge over the moors until the stoving was completed. It wasn't long before Nellie succumbed to the fever too, then after she recovered the tired, weary little group had to set out for the moors yet again, while the house underwent the stoving process once more. Later on, when Bamforths were using Sydney, Nellie, Marion and Gilbert for their postcard studies, there was no need for them to feign tears or deep emotion. For to live through such traumatic moments was to etch them on the memory and soul forevermore.

But troubles weren't over for the Leake family in that fateful year of 1900: Sydney contracted typhoid fever. That must have

Marion in one of her many heart rending poses.

Little Robin Tapping on the Pane.

When the snow was falling, on a bitter winter night
I and little Mary watched it wrapping all the world in white;
Came a little Robin Redbreast, hungry, shivering, and in pain,
And we heard him gently tapping on the window pane,
Little Mary ope'd the window, bitter blew the wind and strong,
Warm'd and fed the little stranger, and he paid them with a song.

Marion (left) showing how natural she was in front of the camera.

been the final blow to the gentle, overworked Sarah. Doctor Charlie Trotter declared that he had never felt as sorry for anybody in all his life as he was for her. And, by jove, she wasn't going to be put through the havoc of having to have the house stoved for the third time.

With all the extra work and worry, Sarah herself became run down, and began to imagine that she could see her dear little Ernest running towards her up the steep hillside. It was then that Doctor Trotter took Sydney aside and pleaded with him to try and get her away from the place that held such tragic memories. 'Try and find somewhere to live on the other side of the valley,' he urged.

Sydney found another house to rent at a hamlet named Gully. A three storey terrace house made of sturdy Yorkshire stone to withstand the rigours of the harsh, moorland climate. It consisted of an attic, two bedrooms, kitchen, living-room and cellar. The house was on the same side of the valley as Bamforths. Not long afterwards, a house at Cliffe became vacant, and as it was only a few fields walk away from Newgate Quarry, Sydney asked the landlord if he would 'do it up' for him.

There was no garden but Sydney built a rockery beneath the window, and erected a couple of spherical stone orbs that he had hewn in the quarry, at either side of the front door. He also placed a stone replica of a helmet, fashioned by nature, outside his home.

Gardens weren't necessary for recreation to the Leake children. For they were surrounded on all sides, as far as the eye could see, by fields and wild, wide-open spaces, with magnificent moorland landscapes for their playground.

TWO

Childhood Diversions

Marion loved to stand at the top of the deep quarry, proudly gazing down at her daddy, working so hard down there in the bowels of the earth. The men had to find their way down as best they could, clambering onto jutting out stones for a foothold. At the top of the quarry was a huge crane, and frequently the cry went up from workmen to fascinated onlookers like Marion 'hey up there-stand back.'

Most of the neighbouring families worked either in cotton, worsted, or woollen mills which, according to Marion, 'were squandered about, not all in a lump.' She remembered the very early start to working days, often as early as 6.30 a.m. in mills, entailing workers having to rise by half past five. Almost without exception the everyday clothes for women were long dark coloured dresses, shawls and clogs. When Marion started school at Holmfirth National Church School nearly all the children wore clogs, but her mother wouldn't let her. Oh, how Marion longed for a pair of clogs, so that 'they'd make a clatter.'

However, her uncle owned The Airedale Boot Works in Keighley, and made boots and shoes as well as clogs. Football boots also. He had a shop in High Street, Keighley, where the footwear was sold. When Marion made known her wish for some clogs of her own he compromised, knowing Sarah's feeling for 'refinement', and created a pair of ankle straps for his niece, with irons underneath to make the desired clattering din. The little girl hadn't worn them long before she had a painful corn, and decided that perhaps her mother had been right.

Marion loved to spend the summer holidays with her uncle and his family. School closed down for three weeks in August. Children didn't have the protracted summer holidays from schoolwork that

HOME, SWEET HOME! (1)

'Mid pleasures and palaces though we may roam,
Be it ever so humble, there's no place like home!
A charm from the skies seems to hallow us there,
Which, seek through the world, is ne'er met with
    elsewhere.
    Home! home! sweet, sweet home!
    There's no place like home! there's no place like
    home!

PHOTO ONLY COPYRIGHT 1909
BY BAMFORTH & CO.

Bamforths cards depicted many family scenes.

THE VILLAGE BLACKSMITH (4).
LONGFELLOW.

Toiling, rejoicing, sorrowing,
  Onward through life he goes,
Each morning sees some task begun,
  Each evening sees it close.
Something attempted, something done,
  Has earned a night's repose.

BAMFORTH & CO.

Nipper, Bamforth's dog, showing off again!

today's generation expect. Happy days flew by watching footwear being made at the works. Marion's cousin James showed her how to make eyelet holes, and how clever she felt when she made one herself. But danger stalked even on bright sunny August afternoons. She was standing by a long row of brushes down at the bootworks, absorbed in watching the workers, when her cousin dashed up to her just in time to save one of Bamforths' prettiest child models from being scalped. Her hair had become caught around the brushes, and James acted promptly enough to throw the strap off before the long fair hair became irretrievably entangled.

James and his family lived in a detached house opposite Riddlesden Hall. One of the maids used to bring her master and mistress's shoes across to the works to be repaired, and if Marion was asked to take them back to the Hall when mended she felt a great sense of importance. There were ducks to feed on the pond as another diversion.

Best of all, her uncle owned a piano. There was nothing Marion enjoyed better than to be allowed into the parlour, shut the door firmly behind her, and play to her heart's content. What bliss, with the brilliant August sunshine flowing in through the windows, to play 'The Fisherman and his Child Were Drowned,' 'Only Tired,' and 'Blumenlied.'

She had a violin of her own, bought from school for a shilling. It cost threepence for lessons at Holmfirth National in those days. Her teacher was a tall, slim, 'gingery' young gentleman from Huddersfield, Mr. J.W. Pearce.

Sadly, lots of aspiring young musicians had to forego the delights of violin lessons when parents realised that they could no longer afford to pay for them. Newgate Quarry 'banked,' and gradually there were only two boys and Marion as pupils for Mr. Pearce.

Marion was then ten years old, and the family moved yet again. This time to Marsden, where Sydney found work, but not to his liking, 'hoist-tenting' at Crowther Bruce's woollen mill. How unhappy Sydney was, indoors all day long, working a lift for taking heavy skips, bobbins, and so forth. It was a sad year for him, despite the fact that he was earning more wage than at the Quarry.

The house at Marsden where the family then lived was part of a Gentleman's Residence. They had use of a living-room, kitchen, and three bedrooms. At the end of the year Sydney was elated to receive a letter saying that the Quarry was Back in Business once more, and he could have his old job back. Off they went to live in Holmfirth again, this time to a little place named Ryecroft, near to the quarry.

Marion had vivid recollections of one of the happiest times of her early life-apart from those days when she played make-believe at Bamforths studios-spent in the garden there. When the weather was favourable she loved to sit beneath the beautiful red hawthorn tree, which came into bloom with the laburnum tree, and eat her dinner before returning to school. A strange concoction her mid-day snack beneath the trees, apple pie and a mug full of Horlicks.

When the Leake family moved from that house it almost broke Marion's heart, when the 'new' people who went to live there chopped down her beloved red hawthorn tree.

Perhaps it was that deep sensitivity for all living things that made Marion Leake such a popular and often called upon child to pose for Bamforths!

Some Holmfirth children.

BLIND MAN'S BUFF.
"I KNOW—IT'S TEACHER!"

Put on Your 'TA·TA' Little Girlie

While 'clothes do not make the man' or pretty clothes, or lack of them, the model, few can deny that the right kind of attire does help. When Sarah was first asked by Janey Bamforth if her little daughter could pose for their child studies and song cards, Sarah used to make many of her clothes. While Cousin Edith, who owned a draper's shop in Keighley High Street, was in her element creating really beautiful small garments for Marion.

'Let her wear the nun's veiling dress,' Janey requested Sarah many a time when a modelling session was due. Cream coloured, it was trimmed with row upon row of lace and baby ribbon. The wide sleeves were edged with a frill, and Cousin Edith had finished off the angelic looking creation with a broad, salmon coloured silk sash.

Marion's pot doll wasn't left out of the fashion parade either. That had a white silk dress with a cream coloured cape edged with swansdown, and a gorgeous crinoline hat.

Other times Janey suggested 'wear your little monkey cap Marion' That was dark red, with a long point at the back finished off with a long black tassel. Also included in Marion's wardrobe was a perky red Turkish cap. It resembled an upturned plant pot, which also sported a swinging black tassel.

Marion remembered Janey Bamforth as a 'sweet person with a gentle voice and manner.' She had soft, medium coloured hair, which waved slightly, and looked to have touches of gold in it when the sun shone. That must have been often seen by Marion, as photographs then could only be taken when the sun was shining.

Janey was the Bamforth sister who used to dress her little model, and coax the child's moods into what brother Frank, the man with the big black cover over his camera, required for his shots.

James Bamforth, their father, founded the firm. Then there was sister Lizzie, and the five sons, three of whom went into the business. They were Frank, Harry, and Edwin, father of Derek, the final owner. Frank never married, and continued to live in 'The Old Homestead' as Marion called the big house where the family lived, until he died. Frank was the organist at Little Magnum Church, and also the choirmaster.

He enlisted some of his choirgirls for the hymn and song cards. There was Emily Lodge, Edith Earnshaw, and pretty Mona Coldwell. The Bamforths were a very musical, as well as an artistic family. Frank was a slim, pleasant looking young man with a moustache, when he took all those child studies of Marion.

Sometimes he went into Huddersfield to recruit actresses appearing at the Palace Variety Theatre to model for him. Queenie Thomas, one of them, used to change her clothes at a local house near the studio. One had to be agile to clamber up the steep, winding steps to the studios!

When Janey married she lived in one of a group of houses called Thorpe Heys, which were built in a field at the back of the family house. Lizzie, her sister, lived in one of them as well. Janey's husband, Harry Sandford, had an organ built into their home, with big pipes going up the walls. There was a conservatory alongside the sturdy stone house, and they kept lots of birds. Rockeries were a feature of the place. In the twenties Janey and Harry had two sons, Edwin, an ardent fan of classical music, and Leonard, who was mad about jazz.

Occasionally during modelling sessions, Frank was assisted by Freddie Senior and Freddie Coldwell, who both worked for the firm. Marion remembered that they too, were very good looking young men, who always wore stiff white collars and dark suits and shoes.

What a pity some of those beautiful clothes worn by local people of that time were not kept, to show later generations-

PUT ON YOUR TAT-TA, LITTLE GIRLIE! No. 1.

Johnny loved a pretty girl on whom he used to call,
   And he thought the girl that fact would like to know;
How to break the news to her he'd no idea at all,
   And he let no end of splendid chances go.
"Best thing I can do," said he, "is to take her for a stroll,
   To propose indoors I think is hardly right;
What you want's a place with no one near you, not a soul,
   So I think I'll say when I call round to-night."

BY ARRANGEMENT WITH MESSRS. FRANCIS, DAY & HUNTER, THE PUBLISHERS OF THE MUSIC.
BAMFORTH (Copyright).

Bamforth's song cards were very popular. (If only readers could hear the melody – as well as the words.)

PUT ON YOUR TAT-TA, LITTLE GIRLIE! No. 2.

"Put on your tat-ta, little girlie,
    Do, do what I want you to!
Far from the busy hurly-burly,
    I've got lots to say to you.
My head's completely twirly-whirly,
    My girl I want you to be,
So put on your tat-ta, your pretty little tat-ta,
    And come out a tat-ta with me."

BY ARRANGEMENT WITH MESSRS. FRANCIS, DAY & HUNTER, THE PUBLISHERS OF THE MUSIC.
                    BAMFORTH (Copyright).

IN THE SHADE OF THE OLD
APPLE TREE (4).

Chorus:

In the shade of the old apple tree,
  Where the love in your eyes I could see,
When the voice that I heard like the song of a bird,
  Seemed to whisper sweet music to me,
I could hear the dull buzz of the bee,
  In the blossoms as you said to me,
With a heart that is true I'll be waiting for you,
  In the shade of the old apple tree.

Hannah Hinchliffe, the girl in picture with hat.

Love's Old Sweet Song.

Even to-day we hear love's song of yore,
Deep in our hearts it dwells for evermore ;
Footsteps may falter, weary grow the way,
Still we can hear it at the close of day.
So till the end, when life's dim shadows fall,
Love will be found the sweetest song of all.

Love and devotion in old age.

perhaps in a museum in Holmfirth. One of Marion's special dresses was a green velvet one with 'silver' dots on. She thought it was wonderful to be given threepence every time she had her photograph taken up at the studios, and Sarah was equally delighted with the sets of song cards picturing Marion and sometimes her husband and other son and daughter too.

Another smart outfit remembered well was a navy blue blouse and skirt made of fine soft cloth, a cream sailor collar with navy blue silk bow. With it was worn black lace up boots with white piped buttonholes, and black woollen stockings. How the stockings kept up is not remembered so easily- 'it may have been that they simply stayed up, for I don't think I had garters or suspenders' said Marion.

She must have looked a real little beauty in her red coat and matching bonnet. The coat had a huge cape collar trimmed with swansdown all round it, as was the bonnet, which was tied beneath the chin with big white ribbons. The outfit was completed with a huge muff, to keep her hands cosy.

Quite a contrast to the rags and tatters she wore for the postcard depicting a little newspaper seller, with the caption 'Everybody's Loved By Someone.'

For the innocent, sweet child look, when she was garlanded with silky, artificial flowers threaded through her hair, and strewn around her bare legs, Marion wore a flimsy muslin drape trimmed with lace.

Janey arranged the drapes and talked to Marion while Frank disappeared behind the black cloth after putting her in the desired position. Both Janey and Frank were quietly spoken, and had the gift of putting sitters at their ease. After ducking beneath the cloth, Frank held a finger in the air to attract the child's attention, then murmured 'Still-quite still, Marion.' He never made the mistake of saying smile, which proved what an artist he was. No-one looks natural with a wide, fixed grin on the face.

Schoolfriends, admiring Marion's hair, used to ask what her mother washed her hair with. 'It's so pretty, like pale shafts of sunlight' remarked one poetically inclined child. It was only ordinary soft soap from out of a tin. Of course, the Holmfirth water itself is soft, and some of the country folk in those days used to wash their faces in spring water, or out of the water collected in the water butt that many householders kept outside. Each bedtime, Sarah twisted her daughter's hair round soft rags to make little 'bob' curls. Marion didn't like ringlets, and never went to a hairdresser.

Bamforths, pioneers of the Lantern Slides which were a form of entertainment before the era of cinema, showed them both in Sunday Schools and at Band of Hope meetings. Seating accommodation in those establishments was on forms, some having the luxury of back rests for the elderly. Janey took Marion to the lectures, and played the piano with Marion standing by her side singing 'Daddy.' While she sang, pictures of her and her father were projected onto the screen in colour.

Janey's Concert Parties were held in the Holmfirth Drill Hall, which today is the Civic Hall. Territorials used to drill there. Inside were light coloured polished chairs. As Marion's father could not be persuaded to go on the stage for the song, his substitute was Albert Booth, who willingly sat the little girl on his knee as Marion sang. Those times the Limelights played onto them.

Later on, Marion used to enjoy going to matinees with her friends. Watching entranced as Charlie Senior tinkled out tunes on the piano to accompany the Charlie Chaplin silent films. The pianist had no need for music, he knew his stuff by heart. Propping a copy of the Yorkshire Evening News in front of him on the music holder, Charlie took sporadic bites, from a pork pie half hidden on top of the piano in a Turner Mettrick's pork butchers paper bag, in between playing.

The music he played had lots of 'go' in it to accompany the shooting and zany antics of the Silent Screen Stars.

Imagine, had it not been for the onset of World War I, the industry begun by Bamforths of Holmfirth could easily have rivalled that of Hollywood itself at its height! And who knows-the young Marion Leake could have gone on to become a world famous film star, like Garbo or Mary Pickford-or an early Shirley Temple.

Marion Leake as a child newspaper seller.

Films made then were shown in an old building at the bottom of Dunford Road. Known locally as the 'Old Pictures.' There, wide-eyed audience were so entranced with the novelty before them that sitting on forms proved no deterrent to the new and magic entertainment on screen.

Later on the 'Old Pictures' was converted into a skating rink.

FOUR

Religious Festivals

B)amforths took advantage of religious festivals to produce Commemorative Cards. About six weeks before Whitsuntide, scholars of the Holmfirth National Church Sunday School used to begin practising Pentecostal Hymns. Should you happen to be browsing round a fleamarket, or be a member of one of the Postcard Societies which are springing up all over the country-or even if you only find an old album in the attic-you could come across one of those postcards.

'Brightly Gleams Our Banner' is one title, with a number of local Holmfirth children portrayed on it. Including Marion in her nun's veiling dress, and Nellie McKenzie, Phyllis Broadbent, Doris Hinchliffe, May Schofield, Elsie Stuart, Mary Winterman-who was Janey Bamforth's niece-Gilbert, Marion's brother, Walter Schofield and Osmond Bradley.

Among the older girls were Florrie Brooke, Clarice Smithers, May McKenzie, Blanche Cartwright, 'Dot' Stuart-Elsie's Big Sister, and Doris Broadbent.

All the girls wore white dresses, socks and shoes. One child hadn't a white dress of her own, so Marion lent her one of hers. A pretty broiderie anglais one. It was on the short side however, and showed the little girl's knickers, but that didn't deter either her or Bamforths from including her on the songcard.

Marion at that time became quite blasé about nipping in and out of coffins. One of the numerous 'props' belonging to the studios, along with the backcloths to depict scenery. In 'The Children's Queen' set of cards the first verse goes as follows:

BRIGHTLY GLEAMS OUR BANNER. 2.

Jesu, Lord and Master, at Thy sacred feet,
Here with hearts rejoicing see Thy children meet;
Often have we left Thee, often gone astray,
Keep us, Mighty Saviour, in the narrow way.
    Brightly gleams our banner, pointing to the sky,
    Waving wanderers onward to their home on high.

This Bamforth card brought together many Holmfirth child models.

It was in Pleasant Springtime
When the Blossoms First are seen
That I heard the children singing
As they played in the meadow green
There was one little blue eyed maiden
Of all most blithe and gay
And she loved the flowers so dearly
That they crowned her Queen of May.

Marion played the role of May Queen. Then, as in life, after the laughter and happiness, all too often come tears. On the second card she is shown on her deathbed, while on the third she is seen in the coffin, feigning death as it is carried out of the church.

Sarah had no idea that Marion was on those postcards until a relation posted a set from America. The photography was done in Holmfirth, but some of the postcards were printed in America and France.

Harry Bamforth went out to New York in 1908 to carry on the business there. They also had businesses in Chicago and Toronto.

Holmfirth Feast took place the week before Whitsuntide on a bit of spare ground in Crown Bottom. A cluster of houses by the gas works, near Albert Mill. A fair was held, and a big bazaar, with lovely dolls for those who could afford to buy them. The Feast began on the Saturday and was dismantled the following Tuesday. Marion's half brother Herbert, who she loved dearly, was then courting a young lady, also named Janey. On Holmfirth Feast Sunday the young couple always had tea at the Leake household, and after the washing-up was finished, and everything 'sided away' it was a tradition that they entertained the others by standing together in a corner of the room to sing 'The Old Rustic Bridge.' Marion enjoyed watching the big roundabouts at the fair, which the children called Gondolas.

At Whitsuntide, the Sunday School scholars used to sing in front of the Vicarage, and every child was given a bag of sweets by the vicar and his wife, who handed them out from the porch. Typical hymns sung were 'Breathe On Me, Breath of God,' 'I am

Hannah Hinchliffe, one-time Holmfirth weaver.

Lead Kindly Light (1)

Lead Kindly Light, amid the encircling gloom
Lead Thou me on;
The night is dark, and I am far from home,
Lead Thou me on.
Keep Thou my feet; I do not ask to see
The distant scene; one step enough for me.

Hannah Hinchliffe, 'the angel'.

Jesus's Little Friend,' 'Holy Father in Thy Mercy,' 'Onward, Christian Soldiers,' and 'Fight The Good Fight.'

The Sunday School scholars looked forward to marching round Holmfirth on Whit Mondays, following Hinchliffe Mill Silver Prize Band. How Marion adored to hear, and thrill to the first thunderous crashing of the drum to indicate that the march was about to begin! At appointed vantage points the group paused, sung a hymn, then continued the hot, dusty march.

Rain on Whit Monday? Unheard of!! Marion certainly had no recollections whatsoever of such an unlikely occurrence. The sun always shone brightly over Holmfirth, and the stalwart marchers, from morn till night. It daren't do any other.

School must have been something of a relaxation after all that energy expanded at Religious Festivals. Back to the cool dark interior of Holmfirth National, with its flagged floor in the cloakroom, the walls ringed round with low coat hooks. There were a few 'closets,' but none so advanced as to have chains to pull. There were a few washbasins and roller towels, but not half as much fuss was made about washing hands after 'paying a call' as there is nowadays. Infants began school life in the downstairs area, then had lessons upstairs when they were older.

Neither was there any restriction on children being brought out of lessons when the sun was shining brightly to go up to Bamforths for a bit of modelling. Janey Bamforth was a well known and respected figure at the school, and popped into the classrooms 'talent scouting' anytime. Marion would have been 'sickened' if she hadn't been among the chosen few. Her heart used to leap with anticipation when the sun shone, she felt sure that either Janey or Cissie Winterman would be coming for her. Or at least to ask her to call in at the studio on her way home from school.

FIVE

Christmas Cards and Christmas Time

When the cold winds of December blew across the moors, and the date on the calendar crept nearer and nearer to the 25th, Marion thought it pure magic to be taken by Janey to the Bamforth home to see the long dresser, full of the most wonderful dolls, which filled the whole length of one side of a room.

The Bamforths gave a party every Christmas for local poor children, some who lived at the back of the church. Most families were large at that time, and George (Punch) was a member of one. They were a rough lot who lived in a tiny house up on the hillside. George had acquired the nickname Punch because he was always fighting. He had two almost equally rough sisters, Annie and Mary. His best pal was 'Jossie Wild 'Un' (real name Joshua Haigh-) the two lads spent much of their childhood running wild up the hills and over the moorland. None of the children were really bad, just mischievous.

So none were excluded from the annual party. Even so, more girls than boys must have attended them, because Marion only saw dolls-or could it be that she only had eyes for the prettily dressed toys?

Employed at the old home was Bamforth's maid, Annie Johnson. 'Plain, but pleasant, with very good teeth. 'Annie always answered the door wearing a pristine white apron.

Supervising the running of the home was the Housekeeper, genteel Miss Greensmith. Whenever Marion saw her, she was seated regally in an easy chair. Marion felt sure that she must be at least a Duchess, for she never saw her doing any work at all. Annie must have done it all, according to Miss Greensmith's directions.

The highlight of Christmas of course, was when the time came to hang a black woollen stocking over the mantlepiece at home, next to Gilbert's. The Leake home was always clean and cheerful looking, but for the festive season it was decked with holly and mistletoe. As an additional novelty Marion used to buy coloured tissue paper from the stationer's and fashioned it into pretty flyballs to hang about the place. They were so attractive that her teacher used to ask her to make some for her too, and gave her a penny each. Sarah hung some of them from the oil lamp, a very ornate affair, which was suspended from the ceiling by three chains. To light the lamp one had to stand on a buffet to reach it.

About midnight one Christmas Eve, Marion and Gilbert heard a great deal of laughing and talking downstairs. They guessed it to be Father Christmas, having a mince pie or two with their parents before harnessing his reindeer to traverse the rest of Holmfirth. But when Gilbert crept out of bed to investigate, it was only their parents, Sarah and Sydney, entertaining Nellie and her 'young man' Fred, Herbert and Janey, Ernest Clough and his wife, to a supper of shin beef stew.

Though Santa was late with his deliveries, they proved worth waiting for. Marion woke to find a perfectly adorable doll's cradle, which, unbeknown to her had been made by a local joiner, and Gilbert was thrilled beyond measure with a toy magic lantern. There were blinds at the windows of their house, which served as a screen for the new would-be rival to Bamforths. The lantern had oil and a bit of wick, and was a Dream Come True. It was complete with tiny, 2″ square slides, portraying simple subjects such as a duck, and a funny little man. In the stockings were the expected spiced pigs with curly woollen tails, an apple and an orange, some nuts and a bright new penny.

Janey Baldwin, Herbert's young lady, used to give the children a chocolate donkey each, wrapped up in tissue paper. She always stayed the night on Christmas Eve.

Another treat on Christmas morning was a breakfast of bacon and eggs-the family enjoyed that only on Sundays at other times. Then the twenty minute walk to morning service at Holmfirth Parish Church, while Sarah stayed at home to attend to the

SANTA CLAUS AT WORK.

Marion Leake and Elsie Stuart asleep while Santa visits.

cooking. No-one in the family possessed a car, and there weren't any buses. Janey and Herbert were mad about The First Noel, and sang every verse over and over again throughout the Joyous Day.

There was a big fowl and plenty of vegetables for dinner when they returned, followed by Christmas pudding and rum sauce. Sydney drank home-brewed beer, in an attempt to gain some relief from the accumulation of stone dust, caused by working in the quarry.

The afternoon was pleasantly spent in another walk, to Great Uncle Alfred's farm over at Austenley. On the way to the Isle of Skye, across the valley. Another two miles each way, but in spectacular, rugged beauty of the countryside it was no penance. It was a smallholding, with poultry and pigs. Herbert, Janey, Gilbert and Marion made sure they were home before darkness fell, it wouldn't have been expedient to be out in those lonely places in mid-winter.

Then, when all were safely gathered in, there was a scrumptuous High Tea of boiled ham, beef, pickles, plenty of bread and butter, trifle, mince pies and lots of cups of tea.

Everyone was expected to contribute something to the evening's entertainment later.

'What shall I play on the violin Daddy?' Marion wanted to know. The reply never varied.

'The Christmas Hymn, please.' Even when it wasn't Christmas, it was Sydney's first choice. And there was really never any question about Janey and Herbert's decision. 'The First Noel,' sung as many times as anyone roared for an encore, and their old favourite, 'The Old Rustic Bridge By the Mill.' Truly *their* song.

On Boxing Day the courting couples, Janey and Herbert, Nellie and Fred never failed to follow the Holme Valley hunting pack on foot.

Marion featured on a number of Bamforth Christmas cards, as did her schoolfriends of that time. Not many of the postcards were in colour. Titles include 'Are You Santa Claus?' where Edwin Bamforth is dressed as a burglar, shining a torch. Tom Ballantyne was the unsuspecting boy. 'He Ain't Been Yet' where Tom is kneeling up, while Marion inspects the stocking. 'Christmas Morning-Santa Claus Has Been,' Tom sits triumphantly blowing a new trumpet, while Marion smiles up at him. Then there is 'Dreaming of Santa Claus,' and 'Santa Claus at Work.' Janey Bamforth takes the part of Santa in that one, and Elsie Stuart is almost obliterated beneath the bedclothes, while Marion was pretending to be fast asleep by her side.

Another sepia Christmas card, where a few local girls, and Marion, had only their smiling faces showing from the depths of what was intended to give the impression of deep snow, had the simple caption, 'A Merry Christmas.'

Marion and the others had a bit of fun with all that cotton wool, playing about with it.

Sydney, her father, was the Shepherd, along with a shepherd's crook, in the postcard 'While Shepherds Watched.' He is also on 'Nazareth,' where he posed as the first Shepherd, with local young weaver, Hannah Hinchliffe, as the Virgin Mary. They used a real baby in the studio for the portrayal of The Christ Child-Edith Shaw, from Hey Gap.

What lovely words accompany the simple setting.

'Though Poor be the Chamber,
Come Here, Come and adore,
Lo the Lord of Heaven,
Hath to Mortals Given
Life for Evermore.'

SIX

'Daddy'

Sarah, Marion's mother, never went up Bamforth's winding stone steps to the studios to do any modelling herself, she was a very reserved type of lady. However, she was proud of her small daughter, when, in The Holmfirth Express, she read how little Marion Leake had sung 'Daddy' to accompany slides shown of herself and her father Sydney,

The audience had been 'brought to tears.'

Janey Bamforth had formed a concert party in 1906, of which Marion was the youngest member. On the pink programme, among the other acts, was printed 'Daddy-By Special Request. Miss Marion Leake.' At the end of the concert a life-size coloured slide of Marion, in nightie and night cap, with a candle in her hand to light her way to bed, was shown on the screen with the words 'Goodnight.'

Marion had proved herself worthy of the reward promised by her mother if she sang loud enough for those in the audience right at the back of the Hall to hear. What little girl could resist the prize of a big shiny red skipping rope, with golden jingling bells on?

Janey used to take Marion to her home to teach her the words, and to play the tune on her piano. What words-words that would surely melt a heart of stone!

For the Daddy song cards the studio had been made to resemble a typical Yorkshire cottage interior, with an old pegged rug before the fireplace, plate rack on the wall, and a table laid ready for tea with white cloth and, poignantly, only two plain white cups and saucers. Frank Bamforth was the photographer.

Sydney had called in at the studio straight from work in the quarry, still in his working clothes, as requested, and Marion on

DADDY. (1.)

Take my head on your shoulder, Daddy, turn your face to the west,
    It is just the hour when the sky turns gold, the hour that Mother loves best;
The day has been long without you, Daddy, you've been such a while away,
    And now you're as tired of your work, Daddy, as I am tired of my play.
But I've got you and you've got me, so everything seems right,
    I wonder if Mother is thinking of us, because it is my birthday night.

BAMFORTH & CO.   WORDS BY PERMISSION OF BOOSEY & CO.

Marion's favourite song.

" *My dear lad, what will your Father say
fishing on Sunday ?* "
" *Well, last time 'e said, ' Where the 'ells
the fish ?* ' "

BAMFORTH (Copyright)

Marion's brother Gilbert, (the boy) Sundays then – what a contrast!

her way home from school. Little did they realise that many years later people would be avidly collecting that and other sets of sentimental song cards once again, and that the small Holmfirth schoolgirl would be appearing on B.B.C. (T.V. 'Nationwide' in September, 1980,) to describe those early days.

Despite his willingness to model in the privacy of the studios, with people that he knew well, Sydney, like Sarah, was basically a shy person, and couldn't be persuaded to go on stage. Neither could Gilbert, Marion's brother. Girls, then as now, were always more willing to show themselves off in public. Among them were familiar names. Blanche Cartwright, Doris Broadbent, May Jackson, and Doris Hinchliffe. It must have been a wonderful artistic outlet in that then isolated country community, with virtually no access to 'The Bright Lights' for such girls.

Postcards were made of a song called 'Rainbow,' which they danced in the concert party. Each girl dancing with a long, differently coloured muslin scarf floating about, while as they danced the limelights played over them. The first line of the song was 'Rainbow, Rainbow, I would have you leave me never –'

Doris Broadbent danced a gipsy number, with tambourines, and there were a couple of talented comediennes, Jenny and Beattie Allen. One of their acts included a very large stick of rock-courtesy of Bamforths, naturally-which they were pretending to be 'falling out' over.

But 'Daddy' proved to be then, as now, the pièce de resistance.

SEVEN

More Titles

Some of Bamforths own favourite cards, featuring Marion on them, and made special mention of on their order forms, were 'His First Kiss', 'Two's Company, Three's None', 'Beg', 'Her Morning Toilet', and 'Good Night'.

'Good Night' portrays her in long cotton nightdress, broderie anglaise nightcap, holding her China doll in one hand and a pewter candlestick in the other. It used to be shown at the Valley Theatre for a time instead of 'The King'.

Too young to feature in 'The Lovers' main series, Marion teetered dangerously on the brink when she and young Harry Marshall posed for 'Two's Company, Three's None.' They were both perhaps seven years old at that time. A later card, with the two participants sharing the same seat, was entitled 'We Are Going To Be Married Some Day.'

No book about Bamforths would be complete without mentioning the major role played by Edwin (Teddy) Bamforth's pet fox terrier, who resembled Nipper, the little dog who peers enquiringly into the large fluted gramophone horn on His Master's Voice records. Truly, a family firm, where even the dog played an integral part in the firm's resounding success.

The terrier was a great pal of Marion's, and both were the star turns on the 'Beg' card. For that one the studio had its appearance altered to resemble a bedroom, and Marion had to hold a titbit up for the dog to take.

She vividly remembered how the maid, Annie Johnson, came in with a real boiled egg and toast, which Marion eagerly ate after the shot had been taken. Despite having enjoyed breakfast at home beforehand!

The little fox terrier was a 'natural.' It's expressions could have out Lassie'd Lassie, especially in some of the more sentimental

TWO'S COMPANY, THREE'S NONE.

Marion (seated) with Harry Marshall as her 'beau'.

cards, such as 'The Empty Chair,' where he stares balefully into the fire while the rest of the family mourn for a missing soldier son.

There was never any bother getting it to do what was required of it at all. It was just as though it knew. The little Bamforth dog loved the limelight so well that his rear end inadvertently appears on a card on which he wasn't intended to be. There he is, scuttling away beneath the bed, where someone had to push him, barely out of sight, on the postcard 'Her Morning Toilet.' Where Marion is pictured preparing to wash her face, bending over the old-fashioned bowl and standing on a chair to reach it. She wore her own cream coloured flannelette petticoat and red 'stays' on that photograph. ('Stays' were the forerunner of liberty bodices.)

Janey Bamforth, out of view of the camera lens, but in full view of the subject on the chair, filled her own hands full of soapsuds then rubbed them over her own face. 'You do it now,' she coaxed the laughing child,-and another winning postcard was born.

Marion treasured one card in particular 'starring' her sister Nellie. Older than Marion, she worked at Bamforths, as well as frequently modelling for their song cards. Prior to doing that she was nursemaid for Jimmy Winterman. 'Mary' is the title of the card, and the setting was at Marks Bottoms, a beauty spot at the top of Holmfirth.

Photography wasn't always done in the studios. A local churchyard was a regular venue as well. Some of the workmen carried the heavy cameras to out of door locations. Such fellows as Freddie Bullock, who did odd jobs besides being the gardener, and in constant demand to pose for comic postcards.

The verse on the postcard 'Mary' is as follows;

> 'Kind, kind and gentle is she
> Kind is my Mary,
> The tender blossom on the tree
> Cannot compare with Mary.'

Nipper, Bamforth's dog.

THE VACANT CHAIR 2.

At our fireside sad and lonely
Often will the bosom swell,
At remembrance of the story
How our noble Willie fell.
How he strove to bear our banner
Through the thickest of the fight,
And upheld our country's honour
Of the strength of manhood's might.

Two cards including the Bamforth's fox terrier, Nipper, from humorous to heart rending.

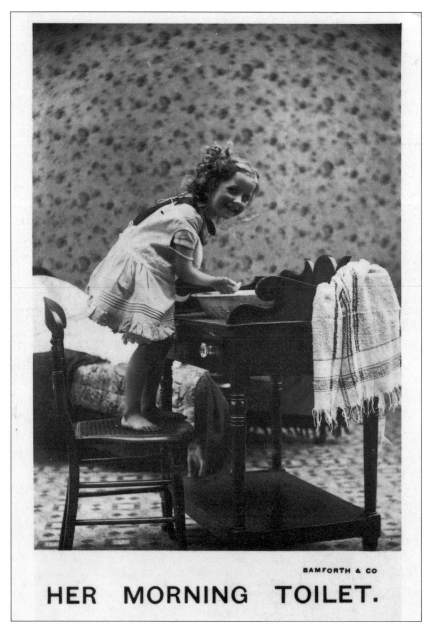

HER MORNING TOILET.

Marion Leake washes her face while Nipper scuttles beneath the bed.

"Missis, will yer please sew me
a Shirt on this Button?"

Two examples of comic postcards.

For 'Shall We Gather At The River,' set of cards, palms and plants were brought out of the greenhouse to create the impression of a garden in the studio. There was a painted backcloth of a waterfall and a river. The emphasis on the majority of song card postcards was on religious themes.

'The Glory Song' features Marion, also Emily Lodge, who was a weaver at Washpit Mill, Hannah Hinchliffe, weaver at Bottom's Mill, Edith Earnshaw, and Mona Coldwell, who worked for Bamforths.

Marion wore the nun's veiling dress again for 'Why Don't They Play With Me?'

'The verse reads as follows:

>   'A sweet little girl of eight,
>   Climbed to her father's knee

And as her head lay on his breast
She sobbed so plaintively
They say mamma ran away from you
Dear Papa and me
And that she won't come back again
So they can't play with me –'

On the card 'Heartiest Congratulations,' the 'Bride' was Hannah
Hinchliffe. Edwin Bamforth her groom, their bridesmaid
Marion's sister Nellie, while Marion and Mary Winterman were
the small bridesmaids.

Hannah was chosen as the Bride again for 'My Pretty Jane' set
of cards, Marion handing her a posy. Lovely words those old
songs had. – The second verse goes like this:

'But Name The Day, The Wedding Day
And I will buy the ring
The Lads and Maids in Favours white
And the Village Bells shall ring.'

Marion had a lovely time on the swing in 'When The Heart Is
Young,' and wore a crown for 'The Star of Bethleham.' She and
other young girls are pictured at the top of the postcard. a clever
device to indicate the seated lady's thoughts of childhood.

'It was the eve of Christmas, the snow lay deep and white
I sat beside my window, and looked into the night;
I heard the church bells ringing, I saw the bright stars shine
And childhood came again to me, with all its dreams divine;
Then, as I listened to the bells, and watched the skies afar
Out of the East, majestic, there rose one radiant star-
And every other star grew pale before that heavenly glow
It seemed to bid me follow, and I could not choose but go.'

Marion and other children were photographed in church-she
wears a woollen bonnet, and a ribbon ties back her hair-as all in
their Sunday best they chorus:

God eternal, mighty King,
  Unto Thee our praise we bring,
All the earth doth worship Thee,
  We amid the throng would be.

What children miss today!

God Eternal, Mighty King
Unto Thee our praise we bring
All the earth doth worship Thee
We amid the throng would be.

Although many of the cards Marion is on are not in colour,
Bamforths did employ colourists later and Marion is on some of
those too, including 'Killarney.'

She had a somewhat macabre-or humorous experience-
depending on how one looks at the incident, some years ago.
Though she suffered with a bad heart, she rarely found it
necessary to keep to her bed. There was still far too much of
interest in life for that. However, she really wasn't well that day,
but managed to get downstairs when she heard the postman
pushing something through the letter box.

On opening the envelope, she found a set of cards–

'Thy Will Be Done.' Showing herself when a child at
Bamforths, feigning death in a bed covered with wreaths and
flowers. The second verse read:

'What though in lonely grief I sigh
For friends beloved no longer nigh
Submissive would I still reply
Thy Will Be Done
If Thou shouldst call me to resign
What most I prize, it ne'er was mine;
I only yield Thee what is Thine;
Thy will be Done.'

EIGHT

Strong Characters-and a Matter of Principle

There was never any posing done on Sundays in those early days. Frank Bamforth was fully employed on the Sabbath playing the organ at Magnum Mission Church on the edge of the moors, just across from what was known as Cook's Study. A monument which is no longer there. While all the children of Holmfirth-and probably everywhere else for that matter-went to Sunday School.

Though few were materially rich, most people at the time were richly secure in their faith, that God was in His Heaven, Frank was in his church, and that Life would most likely go on completely unchanged forevermore. It was only when one went away that any doubts assailed a 'Holmfirther' that Life might ever be any different. They had no need to go outside the place for laughter and entertainment. There was space, and time, for people to be individuals, and Holmfirth spawned a number of 'Characters.'

Firth Lee was of the 'Old School' who somehow couldn't believe that the place where he dwelt could run on well-oiled wheels without his presence. Surely some disaster would devastate the town if he wasn't there to hold things together-? Despite this, Firth went off to America for a whole year, and obviously he fully expected Life in his home town to have changed completely on his return.

It became a well-known tale among the 'locals' that, back in his hilly homeland once more, Firth stood, four square, huge American stetson on head, hands on hips, adding a further dimension to an imposing figure-before the old church. He looked up at it, regarding the sight in disbelief.

Mr Settle frequently posed for Bamforth's.

'I see the old church is still standing.' More of a question than a statement of fact.

Mrs.Lee used to keep a high class millinery shop in Holmfirth.

An old man frequently seen on Bamforth's postcards was a Mr.Settle. He fought in the Crimean War. Some of the postcards on which he featured are 'My Ain Folk,' 'Daddy's Angel,' 'The Volunteer Organist,' and 'The Vacant Chair.'

Once a week, on Wednesday afternoons after school, Marion used to have her tea at Edgar Lockwood's home. He taught Standard 5, and his parents kept a grocer's shop in Dunford Road. Wednesdays were violin lesson days, and as it was such a terribly steep hill to get back to the Leake homestead, this kind gesture was quite a boon, especially in bad weather. Lessons were held in school.

Edgar's sister Ida, and Marion's sister Nellie were good friends, hence the convenient arrangement.

In a small village community what would, perhaps, seem insignificant to more worldly wise types can take on an immense importance. For instance, Marion remembered feeling ever so important going through the Lockwood's shop doors on violin days, and being recognized immediately by simply calling out 'me!'

It was Edgar who taught her never to sit down and read without having a dictionary by her side. However, despite her outward appearance of sweet compliancy, the young pupil was fiercely independent.

An argument cropped up between Edgar and Marion. All because he said there was no University in Sheffield, while Marion declared that she knew there was. Indignity of indignities-he actually dared to hit Marion on the hand with his cane, and made her stand on a form! She never went to the Lockwood's for tea again on Wednesday afternoons, preferring to struggle all the way up the back breaking hill then back down again to school for her lesson.

They don't breed 'em soft, up in Holmfirth.

NINE

Work and War

When Marion was ten years old, in 1910, she was too old to do any more child modelling. Three years later she left school, and, despite Edgar Lockwood doing his utmost to encourage her to go in for the County Minor Scholarship, with a view to becoming a teacher, Marion decided to follow her schoolfriends who were going to work in a mill.

Then the Happy Days of Make Believe seemed Finished Forever. She hated the work in the noisy, crowded mill. There were no wages at all for the first month, during training. And a two mile trek each way to the mill, where work commenced at 6.30 a.m., and to get there on time necessitated an early rise at 5.30.

Nellie was already working in the slide department at Bamforths, where she earned five shillings a week, but not while learning during the first month.

In retrospect, though modelling 'never entered her head again' after that, Marion believed that, given the opportunity, she may have liked to become an actress. But until such a world shattering event as the War, hardly anyone born into such as isolated, country place as Holmfirth went far afield either in search of work or fame.

So, to all intents and purposes it looked as though Marion and those other people whose images appeared for a while on those old postcards, would be forgotten. Hidden away, none of them even named, in Granny's old album, to be brought out to show visitors when they came to tea.

As happened in the Leake family.

Meanwhile, during the war itself, Bamforths went on producing sentimental cards, now frequently with a 'war' theme.

GOD BLESS MY SOLDIER DADDY (1).

A little girl said to her mother, "Mammy, dear, why do you sigh?
Whenever I speak of dear Daddy you always begin to cry;"
"Your Dad is a soldier," the mother replied, "He was call'd to
the war yesterday,"
The little girl knelt by her mother's side, and pray'd in her sweet
childish way.

BAMFORTH COPYRIGHT.   BY KIND PERMISSION OF E. MARKS & SONS, E.C.

Gertrude Middleton was a child model in many of the 'war' theme cards.

71

And there were new schoolchildren growing up to model for them. One of them was Gertrude Middleton, who's dad was a parcel agent for the railway.

Mr. Middleton frequently collected postcards from Bamforth's for deliveries. In the evenings he was manager of the Holmfirth cinema. He and his wife had three children, Gertrude, Walter and Marion-obviously a popular name round that period! The family lived near Bamforths studio in a little house in Transfer Terrace, Hey Gap.

As with Marion Leake, Gilbert and Nellie in earlier years, Frank Bamforth often had 'just the right job for you, Gertrude-go and tell your mother you're going to play at Uncle Frank's.'

Though the children wore ordinary school clothes for photographs, Walter once insisted on wearing his russet brown Sunday best suit, because it was the only one he possessed. His grandmother made his school clothes, and he was far from enchanted with them. Walter's childhood face lives on in some of the postcards sent to cheer the soldiers of the First World War. With such verses as these–

> 'O God, please bless our Daddy brave
> Who's more than we can tell
> To Mam and us-and keep him safe
> From every shot and shell;
> And when he's won the great big war
> Please send him back, quite well.'

And another, entitled 'Loving Thoughts of Dad.'

Strange how the 'Daddy' complex still lived on, into the war era.

Occasionally Gertrude had to wear a voluminous flannelette nightgown, lent by Bamforth's. She recalls, as did Marion, that the studio was short of no props whatsoever, and it seemed to her an Aladdin's cave.

If Frank Bamforth needed a laughing child study he sent for Alf Foy, a local comedian, who used to stand on his head while the shot was taken. Alf claimed that as a boy he had danced with Charlie Chaplin.

Loving Thoughts of Dad.

We miss you, Daddy, ever so,
     But you are out to fight the foe;
Oh, we would be brave soldiers. too,
And grow up, Daddy, just like you.

—MADELEINE ST. CLAIR.

Left to right: Marion, Walter and Gertrude Middleton.

A popular Christmas card of that era featuring Gertrude was headed 'Fondest Love to Dad this Xmas Tide.' It read:

'God, please bless my parents dear
This Christmas and throughout the year
And bless me too, for oh we three are such a happy family
And in thine own good time O Lord
Send back my Daddy from Abroad
We love each other so, we three, And we
would e'er together be
Grant too, Good Lord, while he is there, an
answer to my daily prayer
That he may safe and happy be-and feel
thou'st heard my prayer to Thee.'

Still in sentimental mood was the card bearing the words of the song 'Little Grey Home in the West.' Gertrude wore her best dress for that one, but her white pantaloons are showing beneath her long skirt. With her was a school friend, Violet Reynolds.

Gertrude found that posing wasn't always a weepy affair. The children had great fun watching some of the early films being made. Once, a settee in a field had petrol poured over it, and was then set alight. And the Holmfirth fire brigade came racing to put it out.

A painted backcloth of a 'mock up' of a house with painted cloth windows was set up in the same field. Some Bamforth employees and four or five local people acted as though the house was on fire. There were real flames, but they did not actually go near enough to touch the 'house.'

Supposedly terrified escapees leapt through the windows, then ran round to the back and jumped out again, because there was a shortage of actors for that particular scene.

The village blacksmith, Fred Bullock, often posed for comic cards.

When Bamforths decided to make a film about the Suffragettes, their staff went round the village knocking on doors, trying to enlist female 'extras.'

74

WHEN DADDY COMES HOME (1).

How long ago is it now, mother, since daddy first went away?
It seems such ages to me. dear, for I'm missing him every day;
And when, with bugles, and drums that beat, the soldiers come marching by,
I think of him and I try to cheer, yet somehow I want to cry.

BAMFORTH (COPYRIGHT).   BY KIND PERMISSION OF MESSRS. ASCHERBERG, HOPWOOD & CREW, LTD.

The child model, Gertrude Middleton (later, Mrs. Lewis).

Each volunteer was promised a shilling. A shilling was worth fish and chips 'four times' in those days, and a promise of being able to buy a good tea was a real inducement to the ladies of Holmfirth. No training was required, all they needed to do was to wear ordinary clothes, and maybe a shawl, and walk in a group from Holmfirth station down past the studio.

Gertrude's mother was also invited to partake in the Suffragette film, but her husband had heard a rumour that there was going to be more to it than they thought. So Mrs. Middleton refused to be a film star, and earn herself a shilling. She later boasted that she had come off best after all.

For as the local women marched past Bamforth's studios it was the cue for hoses to be played on the unsuspecting group-and they scattered in soaked disarray. Quite unrehearsed, but a marvellous show of panic! Just what those early film makers had hoped for!

Once, when a young girl was seen crouching on the church steps, the picture of misery, nobody bothered to ask her what was wrong. For the locals assumed, and rightly, that it was 'nobbut Bamforth's, filming again.'

The girl was supposed to be waiting for her drunken parents to emerge from the public house.

One day a neighbour's little girl asked, 'Mrs. Lewis (Gertrude's married name) 'what did you look like when you were a little girl?' The child was fascinated to see the old picture postcards. Few children in those days could have afforded to have their photographs taken. How lucky were Marion and Gertrude, who had such marvellous child studies of themselves to show! There was the time too, when Gertrude happened to be in Liverpool with her mother. They were in a postcard shop, and a gentleman was browsing through some cards. Gertrude spied herself as a child on one and couldn't resist urging the fellow to 'buy that one-it's me.' And he did.

TEN

The Media finds Marion

Meanwhile, Marion, Nellie, Gilbert and their friends had married and settled down to 'ordinary' life. Up at Bamforths 'live' models had been superseded by artists and the reign of the comic cards and 'views' took over. Arnold Taylor among the more well known artists.

Then came 1970 and the year of the Bamforth Centenary. Marion the one time child model was by then a still attractive, elegant lady of seventy living on Wakefield Road, Dalton, near Huddersfield.

Occasionally she used to bring out her album of postcards, nostalgically recalling the days when she was a little girl modelling for Bamforths of Holmfirth. Just to show her friends. Little realizing that fame was about to be thrust upon her at that time of life.

One day she went to Knaresborough for an outing with a friend, and happened to be browsing in a shop belonging to a Mr. Alderton, who had written a book about Bamforths. When Marion's friend said that one of the very first models was standing before him, he was astounded and delighted, and they struck up an animated conversation.

It wasn't long before the Press found out about Marion, *The Yorkshire Post* and *Daily Mail* heard about her from the last owner of the firm, Derek Bamforth. Letters poured into her home by every post from all kinds of interesting people. Soon even national newspapers were making a beeline for her door to look at her albums.

In 1971 Marion accompanied a friend to a local Spiritualist Church. The Speaker selected Marion for a message. Did Marion know anything about a gentleman in uniform-a major?

Marion Barrowclough (nee Leake) with an example from her modelling.

The card that sparked a new interest in Marion. Early Bamforth cards became collectors' items.

Little did Marion know, but lying in Huddersfield G.P.O. was a letter addressed to her from a Major Scherer, retired from the U.S.A. airforce. The Major wrote that he had a large collection of Bamforth song cards, and would like her help in trying to assist him to complete some sets. He had come across a certain card from England showing little Marion Leake on a postcard entitled 'Good Night.' Would she be so kind, if she had a spare one available, to autograph it and send it to him?

A whole new world of interest began to open up. Marion started visiting fleamarkets, antique shops, searching for more cards bearing her photograph. The friendly correspondence between her and the Major flourished, though they never met.

Major Scherer had formed a Bamforth Study Group, his aim being to see his beloved collection in a museum, preferably in their rightful place of origin-Holmfirth. He wished future generations to know about the cards and the lives of the people who posed for them.

In 1974 Marion was shown a cutting from a local newspaper, advertising a meeting to be held by the Bradford Postcard Society. An invitation to attend was sent to her, as well as five more postcards to add to her collection featuring herself when young. She was overwhelmed by the ecstatic welcome members extended to her on learning that here was someone who had actually modelled for some of their treasured postcards.

A gentleman divulged that he had been an avid collector for many years, and gave lantern lectures showing old Bamforth slides. Perhaps Mrs. Barrowclough would be able to help him identify some of the people on the slides –?

Marion became a member of Bradford Postcard Society, making hosts of new friends. A keen interest in a subject makes life full of exciting projects. (Other widows and widowers take note!) It was then that Marion thought why not form a Postcard Society in Huddersfield?

A notice was put in the local Examiner newspaper. A meeting to be held at her home, Wakefield Road, Dalton. Marion was amazed at how many people turned up, full of enthusiasm. The Huddersfield Postcard Society still meets, but now in the Albert Hotel, Victoria Lane, every second Wednesday of the month.

Huddersfield Postcard Society, February 1980. Hazel and Granville Wheeler next to Marion Barrowclough, celebrating her 80th Birthday.

The March meeting in 1987 concerned a preview of the then newly formed Holmfirth Postcard Museum, above Holmfirth Library. The then B.B.C T.V.weather forecaster, Ian McCaskill, a keen collector of comic postcards, was the official opener.

Marion, who died in October 1983, would have been delighted. Huddersfield Postcard Society celebrated her 80th. birthday (February 23rd. 1980) with a party and iced cake at the meeting. Singing 'Happy Birthday' to their most celebrated member. At that time the Scherer Collection had been temporarily housed in the Huddersfield Art Gallery in the Public Library.

A film made about 'Marion at Bamforths' is included in the National Film Archives in London, for as long as they exist. On it, Marion can be heard once again saying the words of her favourite song-'Daddy.'

In the September of 1980 there was more excitement when Marion and that other Bamforth model of slightly later vintage, Gertrude Lewis, nee Middleton, both appeared on B.B.C.I. evening

81

Ian McCaskill opening the Holmfirth Postcard Museum.

programme, 'Nationwide.' Followed in 1983 when Marion finally appeared in The Magic Lantern Show on B.B.C.-T.V.

The manner in which Marion Barrowclough's life in later years went on belies the words of the hymn for which she posed when a small girl at Bamforths;

> 'Abide with me.'
> Swift to it's close ebbs out Life's little day;
> Earth's joys grow dim, its glories pass away,
> Change and decay in all around I see;
> O Thou who Changest not, abide with me.

Certainly Earth's joys only grew brighter for Marion, once Bamforth of Holmfirth's most wanted child model of pre-world war I years.

She must surely have realised that, to quote the words on another of her postcards–

> 'Everybody's Loved by Someone.'

ABIDE WITH ME.

Swift to its close ebbs out life's little day ;

Earth's joys grow dim, its glories pass away ;

Change and decay in all around I see ;

O Thou Who changest not, abide with me !

Marion the child model.

ELEVEN
Annie, The Barber's Daughter

Even before Marion Leake was modelling for Bamforths, another Holmfirth girl, Annie Hinchliffe, had captured the photographic interest of Frank Bamforth.

Annie was born on 18th. August, 1893, at Yew Tree, Holmbridge. Her father owned a Gents' Hairdressing business in Upper Bridge. Frank Bamforth used to go there for a penny weekly shave, and twopenny haircut when necessary.

Private customers of the barber had their own shaving mugs with individual names on. Displayed on a ledge in the shop. Where there was always a delightful aroma of lavender and shaving soap.

Mr. Hinchliffe was busy until midnight on Saturdays. Some fastidious customers having a shave in the morning and another at night, in order to be ready for chapel next morning. Home life was strict but happy. The children weren't allowed to use bad language-or broad Yorkshire. Mrs. Hinchliffe prepared a huge rice pudding every day for her children, Allen, Annie, Doris, Edith, Frank and Eliza.

A cousin kept a butcher shop opposite, so they enjoyed lots of stews. Mrs. Hinchliffe made bread, kneeding it, then Annie took it down to Pyrah's bakehouse to be baked. It was carried in a clothes basket, one of those wicker ones, wrapped in a clean cloth.

On the day that Mrs. Hinchliffe married, the choir of Dam Head Chapel sang their interpretation of a well known song-'Sweet Lass of Hinchliffe Mill' after the ceremony instead of Richmond Hill.

Then all the choir accompanied the Happy Couple for the honeymoon trip on a wagonette outing over the Strynes, near Sheffield.

Annie used to be an expert skater. Learning on the school pathway wearing clogs.

A beautiful photograph of Annie and her sister Doris, taken by Frank Bamforth, gained First Prize at a London Photographic Exhibition years ago. Later it hung in the studio for a long time. Finally Frank gave it to Annie's mother. Doris lost her copy in the Holmfirth flood of 1944, at Whitsuntide.

A copy was hung in the Holmfirth Postcard Museum and when that closed, transferred to Holmfirth Picture House as it used to be.

A postcard with a photograph of Annie shows her in bed, while the 'doctor' Teddy Bamforth, takes her pulse. Another song card was Children's Praises, featuring Harold Crooks, Percy and Eunice Haigh, Edith and 'Dot' Stuart, Willis Firth, Maggie Washington and Annie Beardsall.

> Then there was 'Jesus High In Glory'-
> Lend a listening ear,
> When we bow before Thee
> Children's praises hear.

During one modelling session Annie and some other local children were pretending to be begging at someone's door. Frank Bamforth had given them bread, to appear as if they had had it given. By the time the sun emerged from the clouds to enable the shot to be taken, there was no bread-the hungry children had eaten it all. They were given threepence every time they modelled.

Annie used to have singing lessons at a shilling an hour in what began as a piano shop. Her teacher, Annie Brook, hired a room there. As she progressed, Annie did a great deal of singing at local concerts. And was thrilled to be chosen as Snow White at Holmfirth National Sunday School concert.

When thirteen she worked for Bamforths for a while, earning half a crown a week. But she heard that girls could earn more at Lower Mill, 'reaching in' so Annie went there. Work in the mill began at 6.30 a.m. and finished at five. Half an hour for mid-day

JESUS HIGH IN GLORY (2).

Though Thou art so holy,	Thou wilt stoop to listen,
Heaven's Almighty King,	When Thy praise we sing.

Annie Hinchliffe, centre, modelling with other local children.

dinner. Annie preferred to run home and back so she could join in the cooked meal at home.

When she left to work at another mill further away one of the other children, still at school, used to be sent there with her dinner. They must all have been marathon runners in those days! One woman was employed at the mill to 'mash' tea for the workers.

Long hours cooped up in the mill made Annie anaemic, the doctor suggested she find different work. Where she could be in the fresh air more. In 1915 she became a children's nanny, earning £18 a year. At another place later, her earnings rose to £28 a year. During the second world war Annie became a Red Cross Nurse.

When aged twenty-four she met policeman Walter Cooling, and married. After being widowed she continued to live alone in a cottage at Holmbridge, next door to her daughter Margaret. Even in old age walking as far as Ramsden Reservoir most days. Housework and knitting, and the satisfaction of still being in beloved, familiar surroundings, ensured that Annie, another of Bamforth's one time child models, enjoyed a happy old age.

TWELVE

First, to Last of the Summer Wine

One lovely summer day in the 1920's, an angelic looking small boy was playing with his toys on the doorstep of his Holmfirth home when Frank Bamforth sauntered along. Captivated by the child's appearance, he immediately asked the mother of Laurence Brook if the boy could go up to the studio with him to be photographed.

Thus that child had his image on calendars sent all over the world. One, 'Children's Hour' had Laurence with headphones on, supposedly 'listening in' to that popular programme of the time. Another shot, artistically posed without clothes on, was entitled 'Meditation.'

Laurence went to live in Australia, and when he visited Holmfirth in the 1980's, Granville, my husband and I, took Marion there for a re-union, Sheer delight for both!

Before Compo and Co. became almost synonymous with Holmfirth the most famous character in the place was Fenella, the tiger. During the 1940's her owners brought the tiger back from Africa when a cub, and treated her like a beloved baby. Mrs. Harry Lee, who lived nearby, said that the tiger was potty trained. (Nora Batty would probably say they *all* were potty!)

Fenella enjoyed shopping with her owner, and playing in the fields with local children. Grown-ups weren't as keen. When Wallace's grocer delivery boy knocked on the door to hand over a box of groceries one morning Fenella appeared to greet him. He dropped the box and fled.

Mrs. Lee was relieved 'when the damned thing died.' Sometimes she was washing up at the sink, door wide open on a lovely hot afternoon, turned round-and there was the grown up tiger behind her.

The angelic appearance of Laurence Brook.

'Nora Batty' with the author's husband, Granville and (opposite) 'Nora Batty's' steps!

Bill Owen played 'Compo' in the TV series, now buried in the local churchyard (opposite).

Do those familiar with the theme tune for Last of the Summer Wine know the Holmfirth Anthem, Pratty Flowers also? Recorded by the Rotary Club with soloist Kathleen Howarth. Musical gatherings traditionally ended with a rendering of the song. 'Pratty' local dialect for pretty.

Long before the antics of Compo, Foggy and the rest of them Holmfirth was a place rich in culture as well as scenic beauty. Having a Choral Society, Musical Festival, Camera Club, Holme Valley Silver Prize Band, a Folk Festival, with nearby Hepworth Band sustaining the West Riding interest in brass of the musical variety.

Every Easter Tuesday a dog show was held in the Civic Hall. Originally the Drill Hall, where Janey Bamforth arranged Concert Parties, and the little Marion Leake sang 'Daddy.'

While the tourist boom is good for business, it is more difficult for motorists -and dogs. George Smith, a butcher, had a dog that used to lie undisturbed in the middle of the road, in Victoria Square, for hours.

I photographed these happy tourists beingg 'taken for a ride' around Holmfirth.

'Foggy' and Muriel Kelly, with Della her dog during filming in 1983.

Now there are craft markets, a cattle market, gift shops selling memorabilia of the T.V. show-even a horse drawn carriage for tourists.

One of whom declared 'if anyone offered us a cottage up here we'd leave the south like a shot. The countryside is fantastic, buildings have character. People far friendlier than in the south.'

Many agree with her. Including water colour artist Ashley Jackson, who specialises in portraying the area at its windswept, rainy best.

Ashley has a studio in Huddersfield Road, and is always ready to have a friendly word and joke with anyone. On the rare occasions he is not out on his beloved moors, creating another picture. He had a show on T.V, 'My Brush With Fortune.' One of his paintings is entitled 'No Place for the Tourist'- a snow scene.

In and around Holmfirth are moorland inns where visitors can really experience life in 'Summer Wine Country.' Especially if the local people happen to be 'having a jar or two and telling 't tale.' Some are supposed to be haunted, but so far none have encountered the ghost of a small girl singing 'Daddy'

Some of the camera crews have stayed at The Huntsman on the road to Greenfield, near Harden Moss, where sheep dog trials are traditionally held in summer.

Instead of the artificial, la-di-da conversation of the south of England, in a Holmfirth hostelry one is more likely to encounter old chaps pondering the truth that 'flatulence from one sheep can create enough methane gas to power a small lorry for 25 miles.'

Those recalling the second world war tell about the Holmfirth Character known as 'Wagon Wheels' because of his penchant for cowboy films and songs.

During the blackout, not having a watch, he was caught shining a torch up at Holmfirth clock. To see what time it was.

A forerunner of Dad's Army, and continuing the comic characteristics of 'locals' who featured in Bamforth films of many years ago. What vintage!

When Life was Simple, and Song was Sweet.